TURNING IN TIME

POEMS IN
SEARCH OF HOME

DENHAM GRIERSON

COVENTRY
PRESS

Published in Australia by
Coventry Press
33 Scoresby Road
Bayswater Vic. 3153
Australia

ISBN 9780648323341

Cataloguing-in-Publication entry is available from the National Library of Australia
http:/catalogue.nla.gov.au/.

Text design by Filmshot Graphics (FSG)
Cover design by Ian James – www.jgd.com.au

Printed in Australia

Contents

FOREWORD

A poem is a happening! That is not to deny the labour that went into its crafting; nor is it to deny the creative anguish that went into finding just the right words-in-combination that may, just may, deliver to the reader's discerning heart that idea unable to be expressed in any other way. Yes indeed, a poem is a happening; it appears out of the blue. It is uninvited, unexplained, cryptic, ephemeral, incomplete. It is a fantasy. It never takes final form. It is gift, to be received, treasured and polished. It is a fecund happening that births as many other happenings as there are engaged readers. It is an act of last-resort. When all else fails, write a poem! Or rather, when attenuated life stands in mute judgment on grand endeavours and mighty acts, the poem has the final word.

(*You did it / I knew you would do it that way / And you did it again / Other people don't do it that way / Only you do it like that.* DOING IT).

(*When I am old / Unable to remember names / Fading eyesight / Hearing fleeing Especially from high registers / I will read this poem.* MORTALITY).

It is interesting that Denham Grierson's and my paths should have crossed (again) in recent years. We knew each other, and we knew of each other, a half-century ago. That renewal of friendship is a happy outcome of chance and, one would hope, providence. Now, in our retirement, we each find delight (not to mention anguish) in poetry. And each of us, I'm sure, finds in each poetic happening a fitting *denouement* for a life lived as well as we could manage, but not as well as we had hoped. Neither of us (thank God) has much interest in the poem as a means of uplift or inspiration. Neither of us is much interested in poems as bearers of good advice and of earnest urgings to a better life, or of faith or worthy works. Such poems abound. I am relieved that Denham has not added to them. Nor has he been tempted by word-play, alliteration, the formal structures of "good" poetry for their own sake. There's more than enough of that around as well. What we get from Denham is an essence of his life as lived. We see things he has seen. We meet folk he has met. We share in thoughts he has had. We understand the faith that nourished him, and that was nourished by him. (*O to learn from silence / The language of the dove / Forbearance, forgiveness and everlasting love* LANGUAGE). And the fact that he quashes the urge to be didactic; to be the explainer and the teacher, is all the more remarkable, given his long career as educator. I, who have also suffered from the compulsion to teach, find this self-restraint admirable. Best of all, there is nothing preachy in this collection - just plain, honest observation.

Is this a collection of religious poetry? God does get a mention from time to time, as does Christmas and Lent. I suspect that Denham is not much concerned about religiosity - at least not in its doctrinal and formulaic shape. (*Do you believe?' he said to me / Eyes wide, focused intently on / my answer, needing a reply / he could call his own / Do I believe? / Reaching forth I / lit the candle / at the heart of life.* BELIEVING). But, even lacking many of the accepted markers of religiosity, his work is amply imbued with a spirituality of deep and abiding substance.

(*There are roads we must travel / Rarely do we choose them / They choose us / To guide us home.* THERE ARE ROADS)

(*To be in God, to know the paradox of thrall / the giving up in order to obtain / the love, the care of which the wise ones tell / To enter in gladly, nothing to heal our species bane* HOLDING)

The urge to categorise is almost irresistible, and antinomies spring to mind unbidden and, yes, unwelcome. Religious/non-religious. Sacred/profane. Formal/free. Mythic/grounded. Spiritual/practical. All, and none, apply. Denham Grierson's collection will not allow us the easy tricks of made-up taxonomies. The collection just is what it is. And it will not submit to easy characterisations like 'from the heart', or 'rooted in mystery', or 'grounded in experience'. Again, all and none apply. There is work to be done here; no longer by the poet, but by the reader. The poem gains meaning and lives only through the reader's gaze, and the reader's engagement. Then, and only then, is the poem truly happening.

Karel Reus
June, 2018

Acknowledgments

There are a number of people to thank who have been instrumental in the formation of this book.

Max and Maureen Grierson put red, yellow and green stickers on some hundred and sixty poems to aid in the selection of poems for this book and offered advice on form and content with insight and acute awareness of the intended sense.

My wife Mavis, an editor in her professional life, did the copy editing with a combination of surprise, bewilderment and appreciation, along with her customary efficiency and helpfulness.

Fellow poets and colleagues, john Cranmer and Karel Reus, were of great support, the former by support and guidance, the latter in his unhesitating willingness to write the foreword which he did with poetic sympathy and intellectual rigour.

Hugh McGinlay of Coventry Press again proved a tower of strength in the oversight of the project, queries, clarifications and shaping of the outcome with unparalleled professionalism.

In this life, we get by by taking in each other's washing. So it has proved. My thanks to all whose efforts have helped ensure these poems do not fall on stony ground

INTRODUCTION

'Poetry' according to Carl Sandberg 'is a phantom script telling how rainbows are made and why they go away'. That is both true and false. Poetry is in one form an engagement with the Invisible, seeking to give it tangible expression. It is also a recognition of the hard facts of life; at once an act of disclosure, a reaching out in empathy, a sketching of a map pointing to our place in the scheme of things.

There is no guarantee that poetry will make sense. Why should it? It can, however, communicate our human condition even if it evades our understanding. 'There is poetry', John Cage wrote, 'as soon as we recognise we possess nothing'. Poetry is necessary food that sustains us through time, through a journey of dispossession and discovery.

The poems in this book invite a dialogue that seeks to push aside surface debris to capture hidden depths in our daily experience. A turn away from the obvious in order to advance reasons to look ahead hopefully. A quest to identify a source of light that can lead us on.

To be a poet is to be a pilgrim sharing food with fellow travellers. It is always good to share a meal together.

INSIDE

VILLAGE TWILIGHT

A gentle twilight descends, the sun scuttling home to bed
After another day's work brightening things up
Cicadas chatter in the silence, a whiff of curry drifts by
Soon overcome by roses blushing unseen
Black swans making nesting sounds in the wetlands
The hungry belly of the storm grumbling in the far distance

The breathless hush is deceiving, there is here hidden intent
A waiting for, a reaching out, a participation with
That escapes explanation. Surely a whole village is not sentient
Having a centre that goes out in greeting and welcome
To an unknown communication partner silently subject
A dialogue that seeks nothing less than total understanding

A Village is an entity with a diffuse life somewhat definable
The Village thinks, the Village believes, the Village is convinced
Walking along silent roads, past drawn curtains, murmured
conversation

I am compelled to believe it so, counter intuitive to the rampant
individualism that is the credo of our time.
Community actually has entwining tendrils
That wrap around the heart, a chorus of voices pleading consideration

DOING IT

You did it
I knew you would do it that way
And you did it again
Other people don't do it that way
Only you do it like that
I have told you not to
But you do it anyway
You go on doing it
I don't know why I bother
You do it again as always
And I say to myself
I bet he does it again that way
And you do
You do it that way again
It's a kind of disease
The way you do it
As if doing it that way
Is the only way to do it
It beggars description
Why you go on doing it
When I have told you
That is no way to do it
I don't know anyone
Who does it that way
Except you and you do it
That way always
This is the last time
If you do it like that
You will be a laughing stock
So don't do it again
And certainly not like that
I simply cannot believe that
You did it that way again
This is my final word
Don't do it
There is nothing more to be said
I like the way I do it like that

A FOOTSTEP ON THE STAIR

Why do we hear a footstep on the stair
Not from the one who isn't there
I look, more than a glance, a stare
And nothing greets me but untroubled air

Why do we feel someone is taking count
As profligate, uncaring as we are
There is a tally, a declared amount
A growing debt in place beyond repair

Why is it that we look and do not see
A presence that certainly is not us
When it comes to visit, there is no time to flee
We will be asked to pay our fee

So what is it, this sound upon the step
So totally absurd, improbable
It haunts me, this ghostly tap
Asking the question 'Who's responsible?'

AGENT ORANGE

Browallia orange
Bright explosion on the garden wall
Creative agent after all

GOING OUT

There is no way to leave the building
Signs are lost, ambiguous, deceiving
Museum, School, Hospital or Library
We go on searching, undismayed, believing

Guides are absent, advice unsatisfactory Directions
reveal only ignorance in the pointing
Whether it is archival, futuristic or contemporary
There seems no way to escape the building

Lines on the floor, faint, time-worn, stained
Snake-like twist, go round and round again
No bread crumbs, no reassuring guiding thread
Gives promise that we can find our way ahead

Each day renews itself, beguilingly
Setting daily tasks, chores, enterprises most discreet
In the silence's uproar we seek an exit
We wait to listen for the tread of queuing feet

Reflectively we think, return again to where it all began
Look for instructions, read the details small print thin
Maybe there is no path to out
Perhaps our designated way remains within

ORCHID

A gift given with thanks
Purple blossoms resting
A quiet beauty complete
With promise held in two buds
Yet to break into fullness
Biding their time
Waiting for the burst of applause
At their arrival

NOW

Our grandson, nearing four
Has discovered *now*
He wants a cuddle *now*
Now is the time for lunch
A visit to William, play time
An icy pole, and all else

I wonder when *now*
No longer a demand
Will become a moment of joyful
Celebration of being
Intensely alive
Called presentness

ARE WE THERE YET?

Still distance to go
Sun dipping below
The horizon indifferent
Why meaningless time
Travelling to be there
A destination once reached
That is no longer there
Empty
Because there is elsewhere
That promise held out
Never fulfilled
Offering only a place to rest
Before tomorrow's task
The journey calling us
To get there
Before the sun falls
And night comes

PERFORMANCE

Wind-sculptured sand trips me
At the beach entrance
Price of admission
I am instantly alert
A shot-gun type of summons

Immediately I am aware
Of the sharp smell of sea salt and kelp
On the flowing air

A chorus of gulls and others
Practising harmony spasmodically
Crashing breakers lacking resonance
Tuning up
Seeking orchestrated sequence

Red flash of Sea Eagle passing
Foreground and background
In a balanced sync

Green canopy moves in rhythm
Painting dark and light originals
On the smooth sand
Opera, Ballet, Musical, Farce
I am not sure what is about to start

The performance soon to begin
All vibrant with first night
Anxiety and nerves

An attendant brisk breeze
Hustles me into place
Just as well I tripped
Otherwise
I would have missed it

WAITING

Again in a queue waiting
Counting those who are ahead
Looking for a sense of meaning
Wondering what is going to be said

All of us summoned by the system
Remorseless the civic rule
Following the laid-out pattern
Searching for a sinning soul

Centrelink prepares its edict
Anxious faces, grim
Gathered to hear a judgment
Celebrative outcome slim

We wait in a cocoon of silence
Walled within an anxious square
Subject to unthinking menace
Waiting for reality's harsh fare

Fearful of a social breach
Devoid of reassuring speech
I sit upon the judgment bench
Freedom's gift beyond my reach

LANGUAGE

There are many languages I do not speak or understand
Mathematics is one, whose precision and opacity
Confers the status of dumbfound

Music soars, ineffable, utterly profound
Its textured majesty, its balanced sound
Does easily confound

So also gaming language, quick, archaic, new
Digital complexity, rapid, swift and proud
Confusing whoosh that goes round and round

The babel in my head hears uncertain sounds
Words flap away, bewildering verbs, unmediated participles
Abstract nouns

Multiple tongues with accents prime
Incomprehensible, condemning one to ignorance
Chattering, babbling surround

Teasingly ambiguous, secret, shouting out aloud
Even if a whisper, a communicative sound
Frightening as the baying of a hound

We seek Pentecostal calm, a settling wind
That grants hearing beyond the constant din
Silence in the heart of leaping flame

Respite from the hateful cast of blame
Of difference, so total as to strike us dumb
And make us one in our bewilderment

O to learn from silence
The language of the dove
Forbearance, forgiveness and everlasting love

REMINISCENCE

His grandfather who owned a local pub
Caught him as a young lad by the ear
The cocktail bar is no place for grub
Your place is where I pull a beer

There, if by chance, your life is wrecked
You can find solace once again
But if this happens in the cocktail bar
Your life will come crashing to its end

MORTALITY

When I am old
Unable to remember names
Fading eyesight
Hearing fleeing
Especially from high registers
I will read this poem
Perhaps remembering
When I was young and strong
Filled with the joy of life
Not in any way afflicted
By mortality

KEEPING UP

The content of the dream remains the same
Context along with time zones changes
The lost golf ball, partners hurrying on
A misplaced bag, unsure of where to follow

Friends already on the leaving train
Running after when the case bursts open
Collecting scattered goods, the rising panic
The train moves quickly on its programmed way

The flight call, the plane about to leave
Where is the ticket? last call with no reprieve
Hearing the chosen jet's departure
Sitting in the terminal, the anguish following after

Once it was the Joneses
Now it is the rapid pace of life
Complex technology, the phone's demands
Struggling to gain a far horizon

To walk two kilometres in twenty minutes now lost
No way to understand their rapid speaking flow
The simple truth comes to say, somewhat abrupt
The days are gone of daily keeping up

Abandonment, the sense of being cast aside
Creeps into the creases of the circling round
The contemporary flows swiftly on its way
Leaving not just the body but the mind aground

One choice, to go on trying to be present
The other, to rest content at being still
To look around within this slowed environment
Measuring, adjusting to now time's will

Inscape for stillness, memory, delight that clings
The garden where the bees still hum
The quiet bower where the lyrebird sings
The God of slow and present things

STILLNESS

Stillness is not anything defined
At twilight upon the wet-lands
Silence descends

No duck wings flap
Heron and swans now gone away
The rabbits long in bed

The breeze is resting
A world silently at prayer
No rustle from the trees, leaves bowed

Standing in this silent cone
I am sharply skin crawl aware
Of presence, dusk endowed

Immobile, silent, still
Within an enveloping address
A present otherness

I breathe a richer air
Hear nothing, but am full of now
Of presentness, a giving gentleness

No hand can touch
No eye can see
No words describe

Presence is itself, ineffable
Instinctively felt, too quickly gone
Benediction of this dying day

MORNING

Sharp pain, the alarm that heralds the day
Awake, mind and body alert
The day stretches out
Blank page waiting to be filled
Asking for intention
Calling for some purpose
Giving no clues

Its offer does not rest outside
But within
Where resides its possibility
Limited by pain
Which seeks to blanket options

Presenting a choice
Requiring faith, courage, determination
Sometimes the hardest thing
Is to put two feet
On the floor
And get up
Barefoot on a blue metal day

DREAM CATCHER

The dream catcher hangs above the bed
A magic web protective of the sleeping child
Snaring nightmares and bad dreams
Who have no power when brought before the light

Are the good dreams that filter through
True outcomes of this feathered trap
Or are they illusions that distort
Leaving us victims of our meaning's lack

It is not catching dreams that is the key
But creating dreams that give birth to hope
Calling forth visions of a world set free
'I have a dream', a history we can quote

Dream factories are now commercial nests
From which deceiving ravens fly
The clear-eyed visionary has no place to rest
Caught in the snare that makes the truth a lie

We look for wonder that can heal our blight
Dreams that set the heart aflame
Doubting that the darkness flees the light
Believing in redemption just the same

Give us not confining snares but truth that frees
Protective keeper of our sleep
That whatever comes to us within our rest
Will lead to acts whose legacy we keep

A BURNT-OUT DAY

Dwelling in the dark places
Chosen flight from light
The grey skies offer comfort
A sharp wind picking up the spirit
Flat-lined by the calm

A day seeking sanctuary
Night too oppressive to embrace
Full day too bright, insistent, present
We need sometimes the gentler greys
That do not harry or demand

I float upon a shaded lake
A time of slow momentum
Waiting for the silent forest cry
The beckoning of stillness
To renew a worn-out heart

To rest, letting responsibility slip
Beneath the water, a cleansing baptism
Turning away from the weight of others
Listening, hungry for remission
Reaching for the touch of life's acceptance

TUESDAY KINDERGARTEN

The music makes them jump
The music makes them dance
So joyous is the song
They celebrate along
At Tuesday Kindergarten

The sound breaks out in rhythm
They shout and swing in unison
Waving arms, stamping legs
Singing as they shake their heads
At Tuesday Kindergarten

A time of joy with jumping shoes
The fun of being in straight rows
Now bending as they sway and fall
Down to the floor, up in the air
At Tuesday Kindergarten

We skip along the path to home
Full of the dance, the beat, the song
Stories of the prancing throng
How tired I was watching
At Tuesday Kindergarten

THERE ARE ROADS

There are roads we must travel
Rarely do we choose them
They choose us
We do not know the way

There is always an imagined end
Goals dimly conceived
But no certainty
In what we are becoming

Always others are waiting
Providentially present
Who will offer their gift
Calling us further into life

Tracing the roads travelled
Tells a story of loss and gain
Of those who loved us
And those we loved

When the journey is over
It is this giving
That will be remembered
Making our self possible

Looking back is
To recover only a little
Looking forward is to expect
A coming revelation

There are roads we must travel
Rarely do we choose them
They choose us
To guide us home

HERE

'What is the one thing I must do?' (Soren Kierkegaard)

Why am I here
Not just a question of location
Easily answered
Outcome of an egg and sperm race
Triumphantly won
But why here and not there
Or elsewhere
Each morning the same indisputable fact
I am in place

Here, as consciousness recognises
A beingness
We share its wonder
Not nothing but us
In this spot
Given
We are here
Comprehending
What is it that we must do

MARRIAGE AND THE SAME-SEX VOTE

To reach out to another
In love is enough

To commit totally to another
Is a gesture of completion

To be accepted by another
In return is a fulfilment

So rare a gift bestowing honour
Respect for what is held between

A recognition of the offering of life
That gives forever centre-ing

Freedom to be cherished and affirmed
Openly to trust and to be trusted, without fear

These are the dimensions of this wondrous day
This special day that holds out hope

That speaks of being equal, being one
That brings into the light a birthing just begun

SEASONS

There are seasons to life
That have nothing to do with nature
Changing its mind

Nor with the passing of time's carriage
Childhood, adolescence, young adult
Middle years, old age's sunset

School's slow passing
Early income tasks
Achievements on career's path

Rather with impress of the way
The stamp of self upon the waiting clay
A style of being made

Permanent through passing patterns
Memory's gift of what endures
Beyond the time of place

Bound to birthing humanness
In its patterned unique way
Weather that marks each fleeting day

OUTSIDE

ANALOGIA FIDEI

He opened his bible
And taking a knife
Cut deeply into its pages
An outline close to his heart

In the cavity thus created
He placed his handgun
Convinced it fitted naturally
At rest in the cradle of faith

Closing up his bible
He clutched it fervently to his breast
Inner and outer assurances of life
Bound together as one

Unaware or unconcerned
That his *analogia fidei*
Of death and violence
Crucified the Galilean
Again

ON THE FENCE

The old one, white haired, the young one unshaven
Building a fence
To protect the family haven
A shared offence

The young one eyes the work achieved
Resilient and tough
Stepping back relieved
That's near enough

Head thrown back, old eyes piercing
Looking down the finished sections
I have standards, lad, they're unrelenting
Near enough's not good enough, we seek perfection

The young one turns earnestly to reconstruction
Anxious, fearing yet another verbal cuff
At last it's done, triumphantly, we have perfection
The old one warmly nods, that's near enough

ROHINGYA

I am broken, he said
My three children are dead
My house burned to the ground
My village destroyed
I have nothing left

Head bowed, brown skin
Holding together the shattered fragments
Of his life
Coated with the grey mud of abandonment
Crushed by the weight of cruelty
Unable to breathe
My life is over

Wrapped in the mantle of dishonour
We hear pious political promises
Of punishment and restitution
Merciless hands gripping the lectern
Taking the life of the innocent and helpless

This is what hypocrisy looks like
Pretending the rape and burning
And killing does not exist
Branding the wretched, terrorists
Offering us for pacification
The barbecued flesh
Of the dove of peace

PERFORMANCE ART

Immobile Madonna
In the heat
Of the late morning sun
Constrained

White cream on her face
Even now sliding apace
A gypsy girl
Within the castle gate

About nine or ten
Quite tender
Despised for race, for creed
For gender

Aching for coins
To fall into her tray
Food to get her through
Another day

Blocked by necessity
Into stillness
Beneath the merciless sun
When does her flow of life
Begin

LONDON FIRE

Do all good things happen
To those who love God
Images of the Tower blazing
Fill our screens with burning

People die before our eyes
Succumb to smoke's embrace
Scream for help
Leap to their deaths

The Tower blazes
From top to bottom
There is no way out
For those trapped within

The same for those who do
And do not love God
Their fate remains as is
All die together, victims

How then to make sense
Of pious claims
Of special care
For those who love God

The carnage that we see
Has little to do with God
And all to do with human greed
And fatal incompetence

This we know well
Yet before this murderous pyre
The question stands
Where here can God's goodness be found

REMEMBERING

As the year closes, losing momentum
Remembering of old wars stirs
A surging tide of nostalgic heroism
Flows into media beside memorial flames

Twentieth century wars, not Syria or Yemen
Cavalry charges, poppy fields, Kokoda
Trail resurgent, grateful remembering
Heartfelt Australian-ness prevails

Tired chronicles around unhappy shrines
Of loss and death and futile sacrifices
Young men's blood shed swift and wanton
To occupy the mud of rain-drenched Cantons

There is forgetting within this hallowed memory
Of carnage, rape, brutality and torture
Scant recollection of the cost
To those left grieving and defenceless after

Seeds of war germinate again among us
In ceremonial march, and solemn speeches
We hold guns triumphantly aloft
Life and peace are lost upon the beaches

The hare startled, looks anxiously around
Bulging eyes, ready to flee
Knowing no place is truly safe
Not in the grass, the thicket or the trees

We are not remembering but forgetting
That war is an exercise in vain
No glory, victory, or conquering
Redeems the cost of conquest's gain

The mist of time is blanketing the screaming
Covering the pain, the blood-soaked hill
Forgetting and remembering in battle
A constant struggle of deceiving wills

ANZAC DAY

On this ANZAC Day
The rain falls heavily
Not deterring the marchers
Who need something
To believe in
A transforming ritual
That knocks on the door
Of transcendence each year
A gesture that gives meaning
To the slaughter of
The young and innocent

BENT

We are bent wood
All that we are is bent
Emmanuel Kant well understood

Bent or straight we suffer
However made the outcome tender
Either form well understood is made of wood

So we seek to direct
The hammer and the plane
Do not work against the grain

LITTLE ONE

Filled with infectious joy
Unfeigned gaiety
Unconscious beauty

Time will pluck the petals
Strip the leaves
Leaving nothing to believe

Unless the gardener
Surrounds you with protective care
This is my prayer

MORE OR LESS

Today to be acceptable, one has to seek for more
The template here, the frequent visit to the retail store
There the gathering of stuff begins
More goods, more objects, the piling up of things
More clothes, more shoes, more books, more speed
More wine, more sex, more food, to serve our growing need

The renovation that requires more curtains
An action that restores the sense of certain
More tickets, more gossip, one must know
Fresher paintings just for show

More gatherings, more efficacious vitamins
More jams in jars, and multicoloured tins
The travel plans to visit distant lands
More currency, pounds, euros and some rand

So the process grows, a universal law
Compelling accumulation, from ceiling down to floor
For shopping is truly cool and chic
It keeps you well, and stops you falling sick
We seek to buy the smooth, to neutralise the rough
Our lives of haste quite simply do not hold enough

So here the recipe to combat stress
I send it with love to your address
To escape the tyranny of more
All you need is less

WINTER

Winter's song
Is being sung
Around the eaves

No note of bird
Or glint of early light
Rustle of dead leaves

No sound across
The wasted stillness
Can be heard

Deep black cloud
Amassing forces
Low above the fields

Cold damp compresses
The dying struggle
Of the sward

Near the iced log puddle
In the feral dark I huddle
Around a small coal hoard

Hard blistered earth
Thick frost encrusted
Wind swept, scored

The warm whisper
On my cheek
Of God's eternal Word

Beneath this morning blight
Coaxing resistant death
Into reluctant life

Do not be dismayed upon this frozen pyre
Listen to the victory song
Hail life restoring breath

Out of the grey-white emptiness
Denied the presence of the sun
There comes the colour of new life begun

BLOSSOM

On the ordinary road
Frequently travelled
Anonymous green-clad trees
Stand unregarded
Not gathering a glance

Today on this featureless stretch
Surprisingly, unexpectedly
They had blossomed as one
Frothy white opulence
Dazzling in the morning sun

Dark overcast clouds
Coming to blot out
This seasonal glory
But blossoming life covert
Throughout Winter is now triumphant

The inner sap, essential meaning
Giving birth to promise deep delved
Unconquerably
The slow growth to beauty
That is ourselves

ALONE

It is loneliness that has her set her boundaries
With no one else to make her life secure
Repetition in the pattern of her actions
An eye to that which makes her feel assured

The gratitude of being included, welcomed
Delight in hugs, infrequent human touch
A smile of happiness at special food provided
Pleasure in the drive and shadowed walk

She talks with wisdom in the telling
Wrung from a life of pain and tears
There is no sense of victim-hood or pity
Integrity like polished fine-grained wood

In her time no chance of education
A woman after all that had no claim
Self-deprecating of her lack of knowledge
Not conscious of her inner light and blessed name

Together we lift her cases and possessions
Fold up the iridescent walking frame
The eyes just for a moment anxious
Today she travels home to be alone again

There is here an undiminished courage
That faces life without a special plea
Acceptance with a full heart overflowing
A gentle gladness at the right to be

The poignancy of this last parting
Helplessness before the stubborn facts
Redeemed by her warm chuckling laughter
Alone, still travelling on her journey's quest

OUTREACH

Feeling in time's trickle
With a burning hope
The touch of Spirit

In the cracks of space
A tendril trace of
Love's embrace

Upon the cliff top
Buffeted by wind
What makes us sing

In silence's grasp
That softly speaks
Meaning at last

Being above
Mere flesh and bone
Much to atone

The bed time story
Opens up a page
Beyond this age

Suffering pain
Waves come again
Insight gained

In the dark doubt
No one about
The waiting presence

Creeping fear
Moves slowly near
Nothing appears

All love lost
The soul's frost
Feels warmth of summer

COLOUR

'A man's life is dyed the colour of his imagination.' (Marcus Aurelius)

So it is Marcus, for all genders
Life gains its true beauty in imagining
So little of the work we do engenders
An artist's palette for self-colouring

Heavy leather books tell of the lawyer's coven
Stockbrokers not troubled by the sight of black
Bureaucratic pressure, hot as a baker's oven
Sucks out the technicolour that we seek

Rationalists laying out squared no-go zones
That lead the way to dusty death
Scientists ensuring medium brown tones
That blot up hope and take away our breath

Without imagination no cowardly gremlin
Sorcerer's apprentice or knights upon a quest
Heroine in the locked tower, long golden tresses
No brothers with their stories Grimm, no Hobbit jest

There is in the radiance of colours
The power to burst open a darkened, airless room
Without imagination we cannot discover
The bright coloured message of the empty tomb

REFUGEE

Tribal scars outside, within
Still tribally defined away from home
Seeking to begin again, infertile soil
Made barren by malice, insult, abuse

Daily effort of the will to thrive,
Vitiated by famine in Sudan
Deaths of family in the civil war
Holding together a disoriented band

Looking with desperate eyes for hope
Working as a labourer to feed his brood
School teacher with rejected skills and training
Collapsing with the weight of daily toil

Hearing in his ears the constant chant
Go back to where you came from
Fresh outbreak of despair, new wounds to bind
Unwelcome stranger, in the night wondering

How can we sing the Lord's song
In this hostile land?

THE SLEEP OF DEATH

'Give light to my eyes or I will sleep the sleep of death...'
(Psalm 13:3a)

The light in her eyes was fading
Hard to name, hard to detect
The drugs holding her mind's web
Entrapping her spirit-body's health

The light in her eyes was dimming
The struggle, to stay and not defect
Always on the edge, fringe-dweller
Drifting slowly, fragile, alone, inept

The light in her eyes went slowly out
Why, we said to each other in dismay
Did we not see the mounting doubt
Helplessness breeds disarray

The train she chose did what it must
Ambulance workers found no breath
When the light of hope dies
We will sleep the sleep of death

DIDGERIDOO

Long limb denuded of pulp, sap and life
Assaulted by ants, rainwater and fire
Hollowed to leave no inwardness
Waiting empty for destiny's voice

Deep primal rumbling, ancestral sound
Calling up memories, song lines defined
Breath in nothingness, music profound
Throbbing with essence, generic ground

Vastness called up of stars in the skies
Stretches of outback, red dust patrolled
Forests and rivers, mountains and seas
Beguiling our world into coming to be

Here let the Spirit blow in the absence
Calling up memories, testimony's voice
Centuries of beauty, learning self-giving
Filled with life-spirit beyond random choice

Vastness called up of God's central purpose
Traced out in flesh in the life of the tribe
Opening up truth of life's grandeur
Beguiling our world into coming to be

Sound in the silence, hope in despair
Out of the nothingness self-hood appears
Hear the deep throbbing, cascading sound
Memory reclaiming lost tribal land

FOUNTAIN

Water surging upwards
Breaking into light
Sun drenched eruption

Water cascading
A waiting bowl
Childhood, youth surging

Filling up
Spilling over
Long glistening strings

Into a larger disc
Middle age excitement
Irradiated by things

Filling up
Spilling over
In shining lines

Waiting haven
Gathers all falling
Into itself

Calm old age
Serene in the sun
Slower, deeper

Filling up
Spilling over
Slipping down

Pond destination
Active with life
Turning to flow

Filling up
Spilling over
A spring stream

Glinting in the light
Seeking gladly
The welcoming sea

HOLDING

We cannot hold desired things
For holding does not lie within our gift
We cannot hold the years that our life gives
We hold nothing secure, all that we are adrift

We cannot hold the soaring triumph
We cannot hold the youthful blush
There is no answer on the earned furlough
We cannot hold each passing moment's rush

We cannot hold the memories of the hour
Or days or months or passing years
We cannot hold the love of friends or neighbours
We cannot stem the flow of flooding tears

We cannot hold our slow eroding dignity
Nor batten down the joys and fears
That swirl about our daily messaging
We cannot hold the esteem of our peers

There is loss to be found in every corner
Nothing fixed or final in the end
There is no lasting grasp of all that matters
Nor fixity in intentions that we send

We rarely hold secure a sense of purpose
We cannot keep the perfume of the flower
Laughter lifts but swiftly passes
We cannot keep the heady rod of power

There is no way to escape the weakness
That is the fruit of every passing hour
We cannot keep the distance or the nearness
We have no stamp to set the sweet nor yet the sour

The images of hope, the love of words, the bird song
The smell of early morning wet with dew
We cannot hold the offered good, the unjust wrong
The dust of faith that settles on the pew

We were not born to command the rift of time
No matter whether free or inwardly compelled
That is not the truth that really shines
Our greatness is that we are held

And being held makes sense of all that happens
Permanence and possession is of little worth
That while we seek to hold we learn
The sense that we are born helpless upon earth

To travel, to breath the air, to burn
To find in each day its hidden treasure
Abandoning freely all that we should spurn
We come to understand our true life's measure

To be in God, to know the paradox of thrall
The giving up in order to obtain
The love, the care of which the wise ones tell
To enter in gladly, Nothing to heal our species bane

Only acceptance that we are securely held
Trusting in this covenantal band
That is the promise in all that we can know
Held, our names written on the palm of this scarred hand

JELLYFISH

Jellyfish washed ashore
In great numbers
Froze on the beach
As the temperature dropped precipitously
Being ninety percent water
Deathly cold to the touch

I have touched souls
As frozen as this
Who lay complaining
On life's beach
That they were victims

Unwilling to act before freezing storms
Willing their own death
All of their choices gathering
To pronounce judgment
As the temperature falls

ECLIPSE

Soon the eclipse will swallow the moon
It will be no more
Absence will speak then
Telling us what we need
Exciting expectations
That before we find words
If words are possible
Life's blood
Will call back what is lost
Light will return
In the darkness
And show us
Our way home

CHIMNEY

Embattled
Scarred by wind and rain
Isolated
In the wide barren paddock
Once golden with abundance

Nature has conquered again
Calling up time's battalions
To wreak havoc
Ordering extermination

The old chimney remembers
Roiling chatter gathered by
Warmth he provided
Along with soup and stew
At the darkest worn-out end
Of the day's ploughing

Feeling the family life
Flow up through his being
Freeing itself with homage
Praising the brisk night air
Now all are gone
Beneath the soil they tilled

The outer garments
Of his flesh purloined
Eaten up by seasonal ravages
Of sun heat and moon cold

Wearing down the sanctuary
Of poor, tired farmers
Who knew laughter
And what love is

Wondering, is it worse to be
Useless or hollow
Abandoned
In a timeless land
East of Eden

BEYOND

SEARCH

All things are on fire
According to the Buddha
Or being made anew
According to the Christ

There is hunger for explanation
To guide us on our lonely path
Crescent moon too stark an offer
To lead us to the feast's repast

Behind all offers exponential
That pass before our offered plate
There is a sense of potential
Now to be found, if not too late

This clump of earth
This tiny seed
The gentle rain
Warmth of the sun
All things are one

YESTERDAY

As creatures of time and space
We must start from here
A new starting point
Is not possible

A new direction then
Beyond the fence
Across unknown terrain
Without useable maps

If we come this way again
We may know it as unrecognised
The first time
On our return

Presuppositions guide us
That we do not control
Who controls them
Who gets behind their autonomy

For that which we affirm
Is indefensible in the end
And that which we reject
Brings us to the abyss

We cut down forests
That give us oxygen
Pushing to extermination
In the name of progress

What are the questions
Not yet asked
The possibilities not yet conceived
That unveil a new path

On the edge of the raft
We plunge into fathomless water
On the volcano rim
We fall into fire

Space has no embracing arms
Only a cold necessity

That pays no mind
To expectations of home

Can explanations suffice
Rationality conquer paradox
Theology speak freely out of ignorance
For us to find a new way

What does unfrail look like
What makes absolutes
Seem not tyrannical
In Pharisaism's vineyard

The search for meaning
An embrace of ghosts
Who found out that God
Preferred Word to Gesture

Walking on thin ice
Our one option
Belting the piñata believing
Something is hidden

The oak, once an acorn
May know
The arrow in flight
Tells of the archer

It is a misstep
To claim certainty
Before acceptances are in
Changing the rules changes the game

The injection conquers the germs
Who are amassing immunity
Out of sight
Leaving the heart untouched

No more secure than Bank Bonds
When the System fails
Recognising the fiction
Of legal tender

We do not know much
The little we know questionable
So who do you trust
And what can you learn

The dice and the chip
Have conquered
Prophets have capitulated
Being educated by surveys

When I turn out the light
Will the darkness not be darkness
Will I fall into a vanishing point
Unaware

Remembering the way back
To the beginning
When the world was new
And God walked in the garden

PROMISE

'In returning and rest you will be saved
In quietness and in trust shall be your strength.' (Isaiah 30:15)

There is denial and fear
That real things will destroy us
The mirror glance will overcome
The small child's question
Will pierce us to the heart

Do not make us see
Do not let us hear inconvenient truths
Speak to us of smooth happenings
Prophesy illusions of the way things are
So that we may sleep as those untroubled

If we turn and wait
Promise will creep over us
In rest shall be found renewal
In quietness and trust the antidote
For restlessness and hunger for recognition

Steadfastness will find mercy
You will hear words, to the right and to the left
'This is the way, walk in it'
Injuries will be healed, wounds bound up
You will sing a song in the night with joy

Your heart will be filled with gladness
When the flute plays your feet will follow
At the end of the road
There is preparation for your coming
Deep troubling questions will find a home

I have given up prayers of entreaty
For a disposition of trust
Clear water, stillness, crusty bread, gratitude
Provide the plenitude I seek
Dwelling within the heart of Promise

ABSENCE

Joy has reached its eventide
Desolation unrelieved remains in the city
Weariness rests upon the people and their savants
As with the poor without work
And those idle rich who despise them

No peace the buyer, no seller satisfaction
Those owed money, those indebted
Do not recognise a common cause
Those childless and families suffer together

There is a tiredness the earth shares
Purpose has slipped out of the door and gone away
We are burdened with the weight of things
Possessions and their seduction suffocate each day

Promises turn to ashes in our mouths
Words curl and burn in the heat
Where can we find laughter
Where must we go to hear songs of praise
In order to find each other and the meaning of absence

SPIRIT

Spirit is elusive and fey
Traditionally a hair's breadth away
The beat in a Heart
Heart felt in a thought
Life in its ineffable way

Spirit is elusive and fey
As the wind's mysterious sway
Coming and going
Reaping and sowing
Life in its ineffable way

Spirit is elusive and fey
Via Negativa, Via Positiva at play
Inside and outside
North, west, east, southside
Life in its ineffable way

Spirit is elusive and fey
Propelling us into each day
The vision we see
The courage to be
Life in its ineffable way

Spirit is elusive and fey
With and beside, who can say
Beyond and within
Through thick and thin
Life in its ineffable way

Spirit is elusive and fey
Power of can, do, and may
Justice indwelling
Compassion compelling
Life in its ineffable way

Spirit is elusive and fey
Compounded of yea and nay
The fire at the hearth
The warmth at the last
Life on its ineffable way

CONVERSION

How can one speak
Of the moment of calling
Of gathering up
Into and beyond

No prior expecting
Transparent acquiring
Compelling recruitment
Enfolding profound

Perception's conversion
Reason's surrender
Fulfilment of wondering
Unity's love

Beyond all description
Spirit's profundity
Bright birthing of purpose
Knowing to tell

Staging post only
Journey beginning
Light refracting
In all I can see

Expecting, securing
Searching to find
Knocking and waiting
Clasp of the Divine

Life now given
Life now renamed
Life to be greeted
Life never the same

Doubt's other Kingdom
Love's other bower
Deep in the questions
Found in this hour

Return to the Centre
I never had left
Forgiveness o'er powering
God's greatest gift

BELIEVING

The white bubbling surge overflows
Leaping, bounding, effervescent
Erupting outward, bursting forth
Outreaching and expanding
As it cascades down, emptying out
And filling up, spurt, surge and flow
Streaming, splashing on, carried by its
Own vitality, its inner sparkle

A singularity, embracing all that is
Confining, exploding, transforming, transcending
Splendid in all its forms
Fluent, ecstatic, free
We call it life, its essence in us
Brings all to consciousness
Beyond all reason, surrounding us
With an unexpected intimacy, filling us
With its insistent call, beckoning us on
To unimagined fullness

'Do you believe?' he said to me
Eyes wide, focused intently on
My answer, needing a reply
He could call his own
Do I believe?
Reaching forth
I lit the candle
At the heart of life

CONSCIOUSNESS

Consciousness escapes our grasping
Awareness, intuition, thought
Symphony of complex harmony
Nurturing our human freight

Pushing us to outlook
Recalling back insight
Gazing at an unknown face
Seeking reassuring light

Wondering how we comprehend
The quickening of experience
Rushing to conclusions
Of mythological proportions

Telescope, horoscope, microscope
Are futile in this ethereal flow
The thread of life precarious
Bound to a questing hope

Here is the light, attending illumination
Travelling on a restless, heaving sea
A knotted centre, intent upon untangling
What is and is not me

GILGAMESH

Children playing in the loam
At the Volcano's feet
Not sensing coming doom
Happily at play, not yet complete

The Gilgamesh Project sets out
To overcome biology by culture
Scientifically creating a new human
Who may not be human at the juncture

Bionic possibilities emerge
Organic bodies reconstituted inorganically
Cyborg creatures with a trace of human
Artificial intelligence running to eternity

An engineered inorganic being
Travelling swiftly through an electronic maze
Intelligent viruses abroad, uncontrollably cross breeding
Bringing new life, created to amaze

All this transforming emotions and desires
DNA manipulated, eternal trajectories secured
Setting loose again Frankenstein's creation
Independent, uncontrollably control pursued

To think there are some things we should not know
Is not a matter of concern
Gilgamesh justifies all that science does
But what to hold and what to spurn

Unconcerned there may be limits
Eve in the garden unaware
Unintended consequences remitted
Seeking god status unimpaired

Cognitive awareness began centuries ago
Approaching now its own inevitable death
Subject to our besetting hubris
A Century may see humanity's last breath

As mindless as destruction of the earth
Recklessly we end the human mind

A Century is all we have of worth
What then, deaf dumb and blind

Is it we are just a link
Within a chain now being forged
Into unchained intelligence, objective brain
To what end or purpose vowed

Electronic impulse, endless replicant
Growing into a merciless design
Or can love and care and intimacy
Within the whole still be retained

Strange that within the Doomsday song
The narrative of our lives disdained
Where does the artificial mind belong
Death now an escape from horror unconstrained

There are no boundaries, no redeeming contemplation
Corporate washing of the hands to escape blame
Where is the hope of history's completion
When history forever has no name

All without meaning within our own invention
From what we even now proudly foretell
A species thrashing, mapless, without direction
A disappearing heaven, a nearing hell

Dread overwhelms the hope of glory
Why would a Cyborg tell a bedtime story
Where is the sense of incarnated memory
To whom now can we say that we are sorry

The mounting pile of accomplishments
Will mean nothing to this coming deity
Nor the proud parade of technical achievements
Shining wisdom, self-satisfaction, or shallow piety

We were not meant, I think, to end the human
Absolutising the pursuit of scientific goals

But rather work towards reunion
A wider glance, a restored, transformed whole

Set within relationship
A loving of the I and of the Thou
Our judgment is we do not ask why
In an enduring fascination with the how

*The Gilgamesh Project is a well-funded pursuit of immortality,
employing medical and scientific resources.*

*Of one with other similar projects including Species recovery, DNA
manipulation, bionic engineering, and artificial intelligence, these
are the ambiguous trajectories directed to a new and future direction
for our species.*

CLIMATE CHANGE

Winter has failed this year to fulfil its contract
Withdrawing, withholding, grey eminence in sulk
Leaving the wetland ponds rebuffed and shrinking
A sense of tired incompetence in charge

The ducks lift their feet across mud flats
Swans defer journeys, grey heron clearly lost
Fish withdraw to deeper congregation, lacking direction
The growling grass frogs emit bewildered croaks

Time zones have slowed, all motion stilled
Waiting for the torrent's flow that has not come
Wilfulness, an air of desolation
Cold it may be, but where is winter's song

One does not expect such sobriety in winter
Sloth sluggishness abounds
Empty storm, arid clouds slow passing
Struggling *in extremis* without sound

Where is the always given
Sleet, hail, snow drifts and freezing rain
This deadly lull, this waiting hibernation
No gutters flooding to relieve the strain

Is this a cosmic reproof of our blindness
Gaia turning angry from the task at hand
Strike action at the heart of nature's patterns
I have wondered if the earth is in despair

ADVENT

If the Christ child had not been born
We would have had no need at all
To live with Advent's abstract nouns
Pointing towards a distant cattle stall

The pregnant mother-child waiting the coming birth
Gathers what she can in preparation
Little enough in the circumstances of the time
Seeking to do her best to further safe completion

Living with a promise, long echoes of the past
Thinking of the child who is to come
Not knowing the destiny awaiting
The status of this special son

How she must have lived expecting
Anticipating the advent of the birthing day
Imagining the challenges before her
The pain, the joy, the hope, the unknown way

I have for her a boundless admiration
To be a mother beyond all claim
Bearer of the hope of all the ages
A young girl, limited, struggling just the same

I read the text for Sunday's service
A script to re-write history's page
Expectation of God's coming Incarnation
A child beyond the shaman and the sage

There is here a mystery beyond telling
Exploding vortex we call the Christ event
But in its earliest beginning
A young woman preparing, inordinately blessed

PALM SUNDAY

The donkey carries Jesus into the city
Enacted parable above all else
Absent the pomp, the kingly power
No warhorse, moving at a donkey's pace

Clear change in image of Godness
No trumpet sound, no golden key
A humbleness that speaks of what is gentle
All carried to a waiting you and me

Around us are the shouts of wealth and power
Clenched fist, despising of the least
Yet here carried into the city
History's conqueror on a lowly beast

TEACHER

The conventional wisdom of our time
Power and control
Lie in the instruments of war
Weapons of mass destruction
Threatening to destroy the world
In order to possess it
Convinced of sovereignty

Jesus before Pilate understood
The absurdity and ultimate futility
Of worshipping Mars
Knowing where true power lies
He told the story of another kingdom
Conquering empires
With a handful of parables

LENT

Lent has come again
Wednesday's ash upon our brow
Sorrow filling up
The chalice of our now

A hesitant step into
This season's darkened hall
Uncertain, wondering
What will befall

The rattle of dry bones
The whisper of the dead
We are left alone
A time of fear and dread

Where is the light
That lightens the world
A slow drum beat
The banners tightly furled

We feel the growing weight
Of our despair
But still the sense
This rupture will repair

We hear the sounds of trumpets
Bells that ring
Silent voices speak
A choir sings

But now the waiting
In the garden
The coming hope
The common pardon

A fish, loaves broken
For the horde
Forerunner of a faith confession
Waiting to be heard

BETRAYAL

Treachery is a monstrous and black-hearted thing
Rising from mundane ground with unsuspected depths
Fuelled by hidden sources, many springs
Deceit, like bread must rise, the currency of spies

Mishandling the truth with self-justifying lies
In the moment of its execution, blind, uncaring
Cutting through life's membranes, severing all ties
Rendering as nothing the preciousness of years

Should betrayal be survived it leaves a rust
That devours the shine of the loved past
Wrenching from the ground the plant of trust
Decimating love from first to last

The aftermath, unwanted task delayed,
Evasive explanation of the deadly thrust
The bewilderment of intimacy betrayed
A search for healing, in the suffering lost

As the distance spreads the anger breeds
The search for understanding grows, expands
The knowledge that the soil bears poisonous seed
Only forgiveness stays its deadly hand

But in the dark hours the pain returns
Why was the Judas kiss employed
By those treasured ones you named as friends
All that you were to them, rejected, spurned

CRUCIFIXION

The Cross upon bare land
Prison of a dying man
Splinted, bare, a roman tree
Confronting as we push to see
Here the Crucified, the Cross
Displaying unrelieved our human loss
Suffering, crying out, alone
At Golgotha, Hill of bones
The mortal weight pulls the body down
An outcome for which we never will atone
Suffocation slowly cuts off air
A crowd immobilised, condemned to stare
The spear's cruel thrust
A bet on how long he'll last
The parched throat, 'I thirst'
Blood running down to barren earth
The darkness of the fateful day
Three hours it takes to pass away
What is it here that we demolish
Accepting 'It is finished'

Beyond the Supermarket door
There is a remnant stored
People reach for hot cross buns
Paying quickly, as they run
Music plays the bunny hop
Straggly ears sway and flop
The attendant has rabbit ears on her head
They do not help her hear what's said
'Reach Out for Chocolate Eggs'
Despite the text they break his legs
Juggling adore, deplore, ignore
No idea what the Easter break is for
We are no longer aware
To what does this punishment compare
No steps leading to a holy way
No chance to make it other as we pay
Grotesque outline black against the sky

There is no answer to the question Why
No other course than turn away
No words to speak, except on Easter day

RESURRECTION

When does the exodus begin
From death's nothingness
Out of that stygian darkness
Into the light, a sun shiny day
Stone no barrier
To the coming of the light
In that exodus from
Darkness into life

Where does the exodus begin
In death's killing trap
When the gates burst open
Breaking free from imprisonment
Stepping into destiny
Unfettered entitlement
In that exodus moving to
A glorious freedom

How does the exodus begin
From death's kingdom
Emerging new born into life
Exploding with astonishment and wonder
Beyond all expectation
Out of death's dark tomb
In that exodus into
Newness of life

Here the rising of unleavened bread
Here the crushed grape gives up gladly
Its life blood for the wine's blessing
Here the salmon leaping clear
Up a down flowing river
To lay its eggs against impossible odds
In that exodus
This food feeds the world's hunger
This drink slakes the parched thirst

Here in the church
This sacred place

We hear the bells, the trumpets
Inexpressible beauty in the image
Rose window
Unutterable joy, breathless wonder
Hand in hand, a spoken name
In that exodus

KING

The once and future King now spurned
Has been but lacks a future
No expectation looking for his return
Protection of the past is now our posture

We question whether within history's story
There is a thread that holds all time together
Broken into pieces that do not matter
Overhead the waiting vultures gather

Our species has a built in sunset clause
That we may activate by pushing of a button
But whether a natural or a manufactured cause
We soon shall be a species long forgotten

But just as energy and matter
Cannot be destroyed but endlessly reform
There will be in whatever future happens
A Kingdom waiting to be born

GESTURE

The Priest genuflects before the altar
Beside the grave people throw flowers in
The Undertaker walks before the coffin
We break bread, drink wine
Hunt eggs at Easter time
Open a door for others, lay a wreath
Light a candle in remembrance or in peace

On Grand Final Day we sing the National Anthem
At Graduation the Vice Chancellor lifts his cap
Guarding soldiers presents arms in tandem
Balloons set free at random
We plant a ceremonial tree honouring tomorrow
Hug each other in delight and sorrow
Drink solemn toasts together

Anxiously we throw salt over our shoulder
Touch our head of wood with much foreboding
With delight hold up a Victory Sign
Bring out decorations each Christmas Tide
Shake hands with friend and stranger
Wave a club scarf at Saturday's shouting
Send cards scrawled with an earnest greeting

Completed in the lover's kiss
Compound of all of this
The word is not guardian of human rapture
In the beginning was the gesture

PHOENIX FLIGHT

I hammer spikes of words
Into the rock face of
Uncaring consciousness
Climbing, climbing, climbing
Into life's chimney crevice
Rising to a new birth
Lifted out of the ashes
By the Phoenix
Who with outstretched wings
Carries me to another Kingdom
Where words are not necessary

BENEDICTION

Wonderful to talk with you
Down the stairs
Across the lawn
Along the short shady lane
To the road
We are well provisioned
Loaf of bread, fish, water bottle
Flask of wine, sturdy walking stick
Strong shoes, sun shading hat
You must take your way
I will take mine
We will talk again
At our journey's end
Sit down and share
The story of our life
That coming time of joy
When all will be well
And we will understand
At last